THIRTY DAYS OF CONTEMPLATIVE MEDITATIONS

with the

Wesleyan Contemplative Order

Volume Two

(Teresa of Ávila)

Editor

Don Carroll

The Wesleyan Contemplative Order is an outgrowth of the Spiritual Formation Program of Davidson United Methodist Church

Under the Care of Dr. Jody Seymour, Senior Pastor

&

Ann Starrette, Director of Spiritual Formation

Wesleyan Contemplative Order is an ecumenical Christian Order for those drawn to pursue spiritual growth through contemplative practices in community. For more information go to www.wesleyancontemplativeorder.com

MY REFLECTIONS:

Day 1

The Antidote of Gratitude

"My Father's house has many rooms."

John 14:2

The classic book on the spiritual journey written by St. Teresa of Avila is called the "The Interior Castle." St Teresa takes us on the spiritual journey through a series of rooms in the castle of the soul. Each room represents a different level of spiritual encounter. In the first room we are asked to look at the false images we have created for ourselves, of who we are and what is important. In the first room we see that images of success, control or power were often created to allow us not to feel a fear.

When ambition, sex, success and money provide the driving force for our lives we diminish the possibilities for heart centered fullness to blossom in our lives. It is not that these worldly preoccupations are necessarily bad in themselves, but rather when they become the preoccupation of our lives, our lives become ego-constricted to superficialities.

First room distractions are referred to by St Teresa as snakes and reptiles, by which she gives a graphic image of the power of our unconscious attachments and lack of inner freedom.

Distractions in the first room of our soul may not be limited to worldly external attachments. We can also have an inner critic that has grown from some fear to rule the quality of our inner lives. This reptile leaves us attached to our judgment about how others do not measure up to our beliefs and standards. It is an activity of the mind that blocks entrance to our hearts. Indeed, it may literally and metaphorically harden the arteries of the heart. To be stuck in a need for power, control or judgment is to be captured in the first room of the mansion of the soul.

Reflection Practice: In what way has fear shaped an attitude in me that keeps me attached to my ego's insecurity?

MY REFLECTIONS:

Day 2

Development of Awareness

"Blessed are the eyes that see what you see. For I tell you that many prophets and kings wanted to see what you see but did not see it, and to hear what you hear but did not hear it."

Luke 10:23-24

We remain in the first room of our soul house as long as we stay attached to superficialities that block us from a heart response to the world. Our ego driven needs keep our heart closed. We remain stuck in superficialities and unable to perceive our own faults. Our response to the world is often to experience anger. We lose our own peace and we cause those around us to lose theirs.

We get out of the first room, not by condemning ourselves and giving reign to our internal critical voice, but by becoming aware. We engage in dialogue with the inner self unshaped by fear and ascertain what the pattern of our attachments are. We become aware of these patterns and then we separate from our ego self by entering into the humility of our soul. Here we learn acceptance of what our defenses found necessary to maintain to get us this far along the road. We usually don't like doing this, but by a humble willingness we step beyond the hold that these distractions have on us through our ego, into a deeper experience of our soul.

We begin to experience that there is something deeper and richer in who we are beneath our superficialities and easy criticisms.

Reflection Practice: Where do I have difficulty releasing my first room attachments?

MY REFLECTIONS:

Day 3

Development of Awareness

"Blessed be the longing that brought you here, and quickens your soul with wonder."
John O'Donohue

The second room in the mansion of the soul is where the soul awakens to the possibility of some greater experience of life's Beauty. We are not free of the attachments of the first room, nor even perhaps conscious of the degree that life has been shaped by the need to avoid fear generated by experiences of hurt and inadequacy. But in the second room the soul is stirred. The heart begins to open in a way not previously experienced. There is a shift in the locus from which decisions are made.

No longer are decisions made just in reference to what protects our self image, or pleasing worldly pleasures, but more and more decisions are made from a perspective that takes into account the well being of others.

Our attachments operate at a more subtle level in this room. We can easily slip into the illusion that we are acting for a greater good, while at the same time we are clinging mightily to a way we see ourselves in the world.

The test for Teresa of how stuck we are in the second room is the extent to which we experience anxiety at the thought of losing some possession or status that we believe we have.

In the second room we become convinced of the need to lead a deeper life, but we have not yet become emotionally willing to let go of the defenses we grew up needing in order to reach this new depth.

Reflection Practice: What do I put ahead of finding a new and deeper experience of life?

MY REFLECTIONS:

Day 4

Willingness

"Teacher," he asked, "what must I do to inherit eternal life?"

Luke 10:25

We move from an ego-centered life to a more being-centered life, when we begin to ask the question: "What does life want me to do?" Or, "What does God want me to do with my life?" Or, "Why am I here?" Or, "If I thought I knew my life's purpose, is it today what I thought it was yesterday?"

Developmentally, we should not skip learning a skill, knowing how to make a living, and learning to be responsible for our livelihood in this world. This process of practical learning is somehow a prerequisite to moving beyond the ego's full grasp. But once we have the ego survival skills in place, we all begin to ask larger questions. Sometimes these larger questions seem to be tied to issues of fame, power or money. In that case, the ego is still in charge, just the questions have been super-sized.

But asking the question fiercely, "What is my life for?" is always sure to move us to a deeper level in our spiritual journeys. Just asking the question begins to cut away some of the ego's stubborn scaffolding. Just asking the question begins to move us more deeply into the Mystery of our own lives.

Practice: Reflect on what your being asks of you today?

MY REFLECTIONS:

Day 5

Attachment to Comfort and Control

And why do you [Scribes] break the command of God for the sake of your tradition?"
Matthew 15:3

Those in the third room have distanced themselves from their attachments to status and material things. These are good people, making good moral decisions based, not just on their self interest, but on the interests of others. The danger in the third room is that of complacency. We have gotten on the path, become aware of our ego patterns, and by acceptance allowed these patterns to lose some of their grip. We may become a little self-satisfied. In the third room we can become a Pharisee. We have begun to experience ego-creep.

Teresa notes that many people arrive here and that their virtues are great. But after a while, a settling into the third room begins to be a settling into less. One has given up the comfort of sense pleasures and in turn attached to the comfort of control and orderliness of living. In this room it is easy for one to cling to rigid conservative or conventional liberal views. The third room becomes a safe place to get stuck.

The good people in the third room have given up their old defenses and adopted a new set that are more acceptable.

Comfort has supplanted the desire to live in the Mystery of God's unknowable reality. Often in the third room there is a return to a quality of judgment about others that had previously been diminished.

<u>Reflection Practice</u>: Do I have an easy comfort about the terms on which I live life or do I live in Mystery?

MY REFLECTIONS:

Day 6

Humility

"When pride comes, then comes disgrace, but with humility comes wisdom."

Proverbs 11:2

What is most lacking in the third dwelling place is humility. And humility is the most essential ingredient for the spiritual journey. Humility is what allows us to meet chaos. Humility is a form of beginner's mind/emotion that allows us to have a wider perspective than our ego allows.

In the third room virtuous people often experience dryness of prayer and become more upset, than they might have before, by the normal adversities and difficulties of life. In this room there is a direct correlation between self-righteous inflation and obsessing about small matters based around fear of loss. Fear of small losses, of standing or prestige, of little financial losses (how could this happen to me?), or of loss of control over minor affairs may become a central life focus. A result of an inflated feeling of self-righteousness is often a restricting view of God as a harsh judgmental figure. So in the third dwelling place, more than any other place in the soul, there is a choice made about whether to continue the spiritual journey, or to stay stuck in the ego safety of a belief in one's own virtue.

Teresa suggests that often the way out is an examination of our image of God. If we have begun to see God as a harsh judgmental parent, then we can begin to understand even at an intellectual level that somehow we are stuck.

Sometimes it will be our disillusionment with the dryness of prayer that invites us to look deeper than our own self-satisfaction.

At some point there is some insight, some Grace, which again opens the flow of the channel of willingness and humility. We realize that we must even let go of our ego-drive to move toward God. We become humble enough to step into the uncertainty and chaos of not knowing and we slip through the eye of the needle into the fourth room.

<u>Reflection Practice</u>: Where am I attached to my ego's version of my spiritual journey?

MY REFLECTIONS:

Day 7

Giving Up Our Idea of Our Holiness

"Such regulations indeed have an appearance of wisdom, with their self-imposed worship, their false humility and their harsh treatment of the body, but they lack any value in restraining sensual indulgence."

Colossians 2:23

The fourth dwelling place is characterized by a new deeper level of letting go and giving up control. This time it is not about our attachment to old defenses which we obtained in childhood that allowed us to survive and grow up. Neither is it about our attachments to worldly pleasures. This time we are asked to give up even our control over what we thing is virtuous in our own life. We are asked not to give up our values, but to give up our values as a basis to judge and criticize others. Teresa says that here the chaos of the mind can cause great affliction when we are not yet more deeply grounded in the world of the Spirit.

In the fourth dwelling place we are asked to give up our notions about God and even about what God wants of us in this life. We are simply to surrender to the Mystery of God's love. In prayer in the fourth house we begin to experience more directly the inflowing love of God into us. This occurs without any effort on the part of our ego self. We aren't trying to make it happen. We have shown up in a humble way open to the Mystery of life and life responds in our hearts with a big Yes!

<u>Reflection Practice</u>: What do I have to lose by surrendering deeply to the Mystery of life?

MY REFLECTIONS:

Day 8

Wisdom of the Heart

"The fear of the Lord is instruction in wisdom, and humility goes before honor."

Proverbs 15:33

In the fourth dwelling place, we are no longer pushed along the spiritual path by what seems to be our ego generated success toward our spiritual goals. Rather we are now pulled along by our direct encounter in a humble and open way with the Divine. It is at this stage that spiritual progress most radically departs from contemporary understandings of psychological growth. Early on, psychological insight into our own defenses and shortcomings can be very beneficial spiritually. But by the time of the fourth room, astuteness of psychological insight can become an ego attachment that can keep us from the essential humility necessary for us as fragile, mis-stepping human beings to encounter the Mystery of God. Here we have to give up our hard won head knowledge and hold to our heart wisdom to lead us through the chaos of uncertainty to faith in the Mystery of Life.

Reflection Practice: How am I aware in my life that what I mastered yesterday I must give up today to experience tomorrow?

MY REFLECTIONS:

Day 9

The Mystery of Your Incarnation

"The Lord God made garments of skin for Adam and his wife and clothed them."
Genesis 3:21

What is most nagging on our spiritual journeys is how to continually break down the barriers our ego creates that separate us from God and others. Ironically, the spiritual is most deeply experienced in the material—the bodily sense of grief from loss of a loved one, the physical pain of an illness, or the simple joy of movement. We are all just vibrating electro-magnetic, neurochemical energy fields. The more we give attention to this extraordinary phenomena of our existence, the closer we are apt to link to what is beyond us.

We might just give our attention to that thin membrane that seems to separate us from everything else—our skin. When we bring our attention there, what do we experience? When we bring our attention to just outside of our skin what do we experience as right next to us? How does our soft supple skin seem to rub up against the rough bark of the world?

<u>Reflection Practice</u>: Right this moment, do I feel the presence of something greater right next to my own skin?

MY REFLECTIONS:

Day 10

Freedom

"It is for freedom that Christ has set us free. Stand firm, then, and do not let yourselves be burdened again by a yoke of slavery."

Galatians 5:1

In the fourth room and beyond, we begin to experience freedom. Indeed, one of the promises of all religious traditions is freedom.

The reality is that we are born, we are here for a brief span and we die. It is a worrisome situation. Our spiritual journey offers an opportunity to be free of suffering caused by the transitory nature of life and from all the attachments that we develop to try to distract us from our ephemeral condition. We cling to status, material comfort, complacency or illusion of control in order to assure ourselves that everything is fine in spite of our relatively short time here.

The path of our spiritual journey shows us that the escape from this predicament is to experience life just in the moment.

But to do that we must be free. Free of worry and disillusionment. And open to the experience of God in our lives moment to moment. Somehow we need to experience the Presence of the aliveness of the moment right next to our own skin. Take a moment to experiment. What do you sense is next to your skin right now? If it were a doorway how would you pass through it?

<u>Reflection Practice</u>: Is my lack of freedom inversely proportionate to my level of trust?

MY REFLECTIONS:

Day 11

Faith

"Faith is not for overcoming obstacles; it is for experiencing them—all the way through!"

Richard Rohr

What does it mean to be a person of faith. We are not talking about someone stuck in some aspect of religious dogma, but a believer in a spiritual tradition, where being apart of that spiritual tradition gives vitality to one's life. Is faith necessary? Or, is it not enough just to be a good person and to care about the environment and other people.

On one level that is enough. That is a perfectly good choice. But it is a third room stopping point, an ego based solution and for most people it will not in the long run be enough. Our great spiritual traditions are there because we search for a way to get out of the confines of just an ego-driven existence.

We want to connect with something beyond the experiences of our own needs for security and approval.

What spiritual paths and traditions offer us are, first and foremost, a group of companions for our journeys. We can do in a group much more than we can ever do alone spiritually. If we are going to try to live lives that connect to others, and something beyond ourselves, we have to be in a group context to exercise that muscle. We need to be with fellow seekers.

But beyond necessary community, what does a spiritual path offer that is not simply there to a person being good? Ultimately what is offered is freedom. By connection to our own being, and a Presence beyond it, we allow for the possibility for freedom from our own fears and attachments. We are not being good to reinforce an internal ego sensed need for approval. Rather our actions come out of trusting in something greater than self and the sense of being thankful to have the opportunity to experience that trust. Being part of a spiritual tradition allows us to change the locus out of which we connect to our life. Our locus moves from ego based survival needs to trust in something greater than our own ego. Our courage allows us to trust outside of self. The pathway to that freedom is called gratitude. By being thankful we strengthen the basic dynamic between ourselves and this greater reality outside of self.

Reflection Practice: What does being good offer me? What does being free?

MY REFLECTIONS:

Day 12

Silence

"Of all the religious rituals and practices I know of, nothing will lead us to that place of nakedness and vulnerability more than forms of solitude and silence, where our ego identity falls away, where our explanations don't mean anything, where our superiority doesn't matter and we have to sit there in our naked "who-ness." If God wants to get through to us, and the Trinity experience wants to come alive in us, that's when God has the best chance."

Richard Rohr

Silence is the great doorway to the soul and its connection with God. Throughout history silence has been the preferred instrument by the great religious traditions to tune the human soul. Most monastic traditions whether Eastern Orthodox, or Western Christianity or Sufism have used some type of practice of silence as a key element to allow for movement closer to God. Our current knowledge about how the human brain works also helps us understand the importance of silence for our spiritual growth. The human brain is an habituating mechanism. It looks for a way to create safe, automatic ways for our activities to be governed. The brain does this patterning because it is so energy efficient. When we are thinking consciously, we are using a small percentage of our brain, the prefrontal cortex, and it is using oxygen and glucose at an almost alarming rate. In other words our conscious awareness part of our brains is very inefficient.

What is efficient are those older parts of our brain that run patterns with a high degree of energy efficiency. Like having the computer on rest, these patterns function with extreme energy efficiency and for the most part outside of our awareness. The reality is our repetitive activities create neuronal patterns that run our lives. Because of the brain's hard wired structure to learn patterns, a human being is not able not to practice. In our thinking, our emotions and our physical activities we are always practicing something. We can be practicing patterns which will make us energetic and full of delight at life or negative patterns that make us cynical and unhappy. We can foster patterns that make us feel grateful and aware of the beauty of life or patterns that arouse anger and create hopelessness. The first step in our spiritual journey is often just to become aware of what the unconscious patterns are that are running our lives. Silence is a way to experientially see the clutter of emotional and thought patterns that are constantly running. It makes sense that in activity there are not as many brain resources available to us so we are not aware of the unconscious patterning that is running us. Silence gives us more brain space to see what the patterns are that run our lives.

Reflection Practice: What are the practices that create my life experience?

MY REFLECTIONS:

Day 13

Silence

"For you died, and your life is now hidden with Christ in God."

Colossians 3:3

Something else happens from the practice of silence on the spiritual journey. Once the clutter of activity in the mind, the emotions and body sensations begin to subside, we begin to experience our state of beingness. Out of this beingness arises our connection to God and the world around us. Once we begin to experience internally who we are and the self-acceptance that comes with this experience, we have the capability to experience connection to a meaning outside of self.

Another result of the practice of silence is that once we have begun to achieve a place of internal quietness, we also become able to consciously decide what kind of patterns we wish to create in our lives. The mind and body are incapable of not practicing some pattern. When they are brought to a place of quiet—then we can begin to program the practices we want in our life. Silence creates the opportunity for choice. Choice at the most fundamental level—to consciously decide what patterns will run our lives.

Reflection Practice: What is my experience in allowing Silence to move me beyond a chattering mind?

MY REFLECTIONS:

Day 14

Silence

"Silence is the language of God, and the only language deep enough to absorb all the contradictions and failures that we are holding against ourselves. God loves us silently, because God has no case to make against us. Silent communion absorbs our self-hatred, as every lover knows."

Richard Rohr

Both history and science teach us the importance of silence, but it is only our experience of silence that will etch this learning deeply.

Silence brings the opportunity for creative non-doing. Silence provides a chance for patterned ways of thinking and feeling to loosen, so we discover the ephemeral nature of the obstacles and logjams that block us from our souls and God.

Silence makes us aware that everything is absolutely as it should be. Not in some human sense of what fairness requires, but in a larger universal sense of how life is intertwined and how at our core we are connected and apart of this dynamic flow. Through the doorway of silence we find peace and serenity despite whatever turmoil there is around us. We don't just belief in some abstract idea of God, but we have the certain knowledge of experiencing our connection to that ultimate Mystery from which our Being comes.

Reflection Practice: Am I willing to adopt a practice like centering prayer that includes silence?

MY REFLECTIONS:

Day 15

Being

"For in him we live and move and have our being."

Acts 17:28

One of the tricky things about the connection to our beingness that silence often brings is that we do not appreciate the depth of this experience. The experience of deep connection with self and awareness of and connection with the world and this greater aspect we call Divinity is one of the most quintessentially common experiences that humans have. In a sense it is so ordinary, and often perhaps so fleeting, that we don't give ourselves permission to experience and appreciate the weight and meaning of these extraordinary experiences.

The closest analogy I can think of is childbirth. Nothing could be more ordinary than the procreation of children, and in the individual's experience of this event, nothing could be more extraordinary.

The experience of the Divine seems to always be near at hand and at the same time is allusive. Silence is the great way to embrace the opportunity for an ongoing encounter with this reality.

<u>Reflection Practice</u>: Am I willing to become silent in order to become conscious?

MY REFLECTIONS:

Day 16

Non-Attachment

"Whoever wants to be my disciple must deny themselves and take up their cross and follow me."

Mark 8:34

Rumi, the dog, is asleep on her pad. A lot is happening. The muscles under her muzzle quiver almost constantly, the knot of hair above her right eye twitches at regular intervals. And, although there is the regular rhythm of her breathing as her mid-section rises and falls, her left leg shakes erratically and constantly needs to find another place to rest.

Her body asleep is like our mind-bodies awake. The movement and chatter is almost non-stop, and, while following our creative thread is one possible way to begin to get out of this gerbil cage, there is a path all religious traditions have preferred and that is what in the East is called meditation, or in the West contemplation, or centering prayer.

Identification with the thought-feeling narratives that go on constantly is what the Buddhist call attachment to suffering. Attachment to these stories is maya, that is they seem in our mind/emotions to be real, but they are really an illusion. They are thought/emotion energy constructs that have a neurochemical reality, but they are not us. Contemporary psychology often tells us to "feel our feelings"—in essence the suggestion is to get deeper into the illusions that cause our suffering. What we most often sink deeper into is not the spacious ground of being from which God is experienced, but rather the narrative we have around a particular emotion that has been triggered. Without the practice of meditation or contemplation, or a practice of creativity that provides the same effect, the mind is going to jump into the emotion/thought story so quickly we will not have the chance to experience and release the pure emotion. Rather we will slip quickly into the suffering of the story we have attached to the emotion. Also we will be attracted to the many addictive substances and processes in our culture which allow us to escape from feeling the suffering in the emotion/thought story to which we are attached.

<u>Reflection Practice</u>: What practices am I willing to do today to lessen my suffering?

MY REFLECTIONS:

Day 17

Beauty

"Beauty is the experimental proof that incarnation is in fact possible."

Simone Weil

I just watched the sunset. It took maybe 45 minutes for the sun to fully disappear and darkness descend. The sky constantly changed—a pattern of colors from blue to dull gray, to pink, to crimson, to slate gray, to dark. Beyond the presence of the kaleidoscope of color was the sense of something more, something that encompassed the beauty of the sunset.

The development of consciousness thrusts upon any serious seeker the issue of God. As consciousness increases we become more and more aware of the limits of our own perspectives on reality. We become aware of how we participate in the stories our egos provide in order to let us feel okay, and we experience that there is more than just stories. Consciousness involves us being in those stories and also being aware we are in a story. Once we have the capacity for this participation in, and observation of our lives, the question is begged—what else is there outside of ourselves. There is an energetic feeling that there is something else there. Of course, there is that feeling of the presence of others when we are around other people. We experience the energy of their stories around us, but we also experience that there is more. If we are outside in nature we experience the energetic presence of all the natural world around us, but if we are quiet and still long enough, we also experience the presence of other that is a part of and greater than the experience of the natural world.

Today scientists talk about this sense of otherness in terms of energy fields. Native Americans often talked of this presence in terms of Beauty.

<u>Reflection Practice</u>: How do I experience a reality greater than myself?

MY REFLECTIONS:

Day 18

The Great Reality

"I think some experience of God is necessary for mental and emotional health. You basically don't belong in the universe until you are connected to the center and the whole, and a word for that is "God."

Richard Rohr

Religions have grown up over the years around the intense experience of connection to Otherness, of a peculiarly conscious person. Rules have emerged to try to help others participate in this experience. Sometimes these rules chart helpful paths for those who are open to them. Sometimes these rule structures become barriers to the experience. All of these structures are designed to help bring an experience of a greater reality consciously into our lives. Since the time of Rene Descartes the focus on how to do that in the West has been on trying to understand the process mentally. Much has been learned by the scientific and mental approach to understanding consciousness and how we might participate in a larger Presence. But fundamentally we have been using the wrong perceptive organs for this process. God, a greater reality, is not experienced intellectually. Rather, God is appreciated and a greater reality comes into consciousness, primarily through our emotional and somatic perceptions.

Our emotional system, like our intellectual system, operates on several different levels. Our emotional system may operate on a survival level. The emotion of fear can be transmitted neurochemically to bring us into action five times faster than we can intellectually process the idea of danger. Our emotions are important for our survival. On the next level our emotions tell us what is pleasurable. A certain fragrance may bring a smile, a particular taste a sense of happiness.

Our emotional senses also operate on a third level—where consciousness of God occurs. The experience of a greater reality flows from this consciousness.

Our survival emotions, our sensate experiences and our God present emotions are all connected. We cut off any one level at the risk of impairing our access to all.

Reflection Practice: Where do I let my fear of anger or sorry cut me off from the experience of my life? From a greater reality?

MY REFLECTIONS:

Day 19

The Way of the Heart

"I will give you a new heart and put a new spirit in you; I will remove from you your heart of stone and give you a heart of flesh."

Ezekiel 36:26

So how do we most effectively exercise that part of our emotional and somatic brain that is connected to God. In 1935 Alcoholics Anonymous was founded. Bill Wilson, a co-founder, had corresponded with Carl Jung, the famous Swiss psychiatrist and been told by Jung that the only possible way out of the emotional and spiritual depravity of alcoholism was through a spiritual experience. Wilson in the first real break in the West from trying to understand God intellectually, through theology, suggested to other seemingly hopeless drunks that one should embrace whatever conception of God a person wanted. He recognized that the intellectual understanding of God was really irrelevant because the way that humans communicated with a greater Presence was not intellectually but somatically and emotionally, through the third level of emotional function.

Wilson embraced the emotional path of relationship with God for a very practical reason—it was the only path that seemed to work. The only path that offered a spiritual reprieve from an otherwise debilitating disease. For those in the modern world who needed an institutionally approved intellectual relationship to an idea of God, Wilson's radical idea meant that others would proclaim that God was dead. The truth is that a way to commune with God through the intellect has, for most of us, always been a dead-end. The result of a theological approach to God has simply been that one group has fought with another about who had the correct understanding of God. Religion as a body of ideas has always been something that has separated people into different groups in a hierarchical fashion—my ideas about God are better than your ideas about God.

We now live in a time where, with God of the intellect dead, we are beginning to find our way back to God of the heart.

<u>Reflection Practice</u>: How do my thoughts about God impede my experience of God?

MY REFLECTIONS:

Day 20

The Way of the Heart

"So do not waste time hating mom and dad, hating the church, hating America, hating what has disappointed you. In fact, don't hate anything. You become so upset with the dark side of things that you never discover how to put the dark and the light together, which is the heart of wisdom and love, and the trademark of a second half of life person."

Richard Rohr

Unfortunately, it is possible to relate to religion (not God) in lower level emotional ways that are just as divisive as the theologies of different religious groups.

If the appeal and practices of religions focus on the survival emotional level, chances are that consciousness will stay stuck at this survival level. Participation in a greater Presence, will be blocked because at the survival emotional level we are caught in the paradigm of duality, of our ability to survive always being at the expense of another group. Religious practices at the emotional survival level simply reinforce the duality of one group's perceived better survival odds over another group. Much of the Old Testament teaches a quality of emotional connection to God based on emotional survival.

This is why today, as Richard Rohr has so astutely observed, some humanists can seem so much more spiritually advanced than those who function from an emotional survival religious level. Because the humanists have given up theological divisions they have begun the journey out of dualism. What keeps the humanist trapped is their strength, their intellectual abilities and egos that helped to get them out of the dualism trap. Their weakness is that their emotional software is woefully underdeveloped to experience a higher level of emotional experience with a greater Presence than their own nimble egos.

Reflection Practice: What is the emotional quality of my relationship to what is greater than me?

MY REFLECTIONS:

Day 21

Gratitude

"O give thanks to the Lord, for he is good; for his steadfast love endures for ever!"
1 Chronicle 16:34

So we are back to the problem of modernity. Our egos and our intellects have not found a way to access this greater Presence, nor have religions that trade on the emotional survival brain, or the humanists who have under-developed emotional software. We are left to find in the worlds' common religious heritages, the tools to sharpen our third level emotional intelligence. These are the practices that will make God a part of our lives, that will allow us to live in the Presence of a greater Consciousness and allow the unfolding and flowering of our own consciousnesses.

The starting point is gratitude. Gratitude is a deep third level emotion. Our spiritual software is crippled without the development of this capacity. But even for the most sophisticated intellectuals, who like Descartes may be completely out of touch with their higher level emotional beingness, the seeds of the development of this software are present. All it takes is practice for the capacity to grow.

<u>Reflection Practice</u>: Am I willing to have a daily gratitude practice?

MY REFLECTIONS:

Day 22

Separation from God

"The Lord is my strength and my shield; in him my heart trusts; so I am helped, and my heart exults, and with my song I give thanks to him."

Psalm 28:7

One of my favorite stories comes from a friend of mine who learned about developing his emotional capacity for gratitude in Alcoholics Anonymous. He learned it because he was told he had to, if he wanted to live. And like many of us who will follow a physician's advice even when we have no emotional experience to tell us that it is worth following -- we do that in order to keep our health and escape a potentially fatal illness. This is what my friend had done.

He had been sober for a number of years and was hospitalized for surgery. The surgery went well but early the next morning as he was recovering, he began to feel the affects of various medications he had been given and palpable waves of depression began to well-up and roll over him. He buzzed for the night nurse. She came to his room and he asked her to get a pad and pencil. She was a bit puzzled but complied. He then asked her to begin to write down a gratitude list for him, as he had done so many times before at the instruction of his AA sponsor. About the fourth item, he described his experience as being "as if I broke out from underneath a wave of darkness." The nurse noted that his vital signs which were all being monitored, shifted in a more positive direction. The change was so immediate and direct the nurse was stunned. In her amazement she asked my friend, "Do you think I could use this with other patients?"

Only through the experience of the deep emotion of gratitude do we get to experience its remarkable power. The more deeply it is felt, the more it offers the opportunity to change our emotional and physical realities as my friend experienced, and the more it opens us up to connection with God, to connection with a greater Consciousness, to the experience that is the very medium in which the great mystics lived.

Reflection Practice: Have I used this book's meditation practice in a way to develop my gratitude software? What have I experienced?

MY REFLECTIONS:

Day 23

Gratitude

"And he got down upon his knees three times a day and prayed and gave thanks before his God."

Daniel 6:10

The essential nature of gratitude for spiritual growth is reflected in most traditional religious liturgies. These liturgies provide prayers of thanksgiving at an early part of the liturgy as a way to begin to prepare the emotional software of participants for connection to a greater Consciousness. In other words it is from the place of heartfelt gratitude that we are both able to extent our consciousness out into the world and also able to receive the Consciousness of the world.

Engagement in a place of emotionally felt gratitude is the basic software that has to be booted into place. From the place of deeply felt gratitude one is then able to pray in a way that opens the prayer to a deeper sense of self, to a deeper sense of the Beauty of all life and to a deeper connection to the Presence of Other, to God, to Spirit.

Reflection Practice: Can I step into a place of deep gratitude? What is present there for me today?

MY REFLECTIONS:

Day 24

Humility

"Great science, which we once considered an "enemy" of religion, is now helping us see that we're standing in the middle of awesome Mystery, and the only response before that Mystery is immense humility."

Richard Rohr

The ability to access the emotion of deep gratitude is enhanced by a certain perspective. If one approaches life from a perspective of humility, then one is more able to develop one's emotional capacity for gratitude.

Humility is a lot like realism. It avoids the over-inflation that can go with optimism and the negativity and self-absorption that goes with pessimism and depression. Humility recognizes the interconnection of all things—and the emotional reality of appreciating this interconnection is a precursor to gratitude. Go into a large grocery store, or a market place in Mexico City, or any large city, and we are amazed at the diversity of products that are available for purchase. The efforts of many people we will never know sustain our very lives, our whims and most serious efforts. Not only is humility realistic, it is realism with a touch of soul. True humility opens up connections because it has dropped barriers of protection, defenses that no longer serve, and presumptions that need to be reinforced by will.

While humility is not ego inflating, it is also not deprecating. It recognizes the pure miracle of each soul's life in this world, including our own. Humility recognizes our relationship with the world around us as the primary reason for our being here.

We are in a sense our relationships. From a perspective of humility we are most right-sized in our relationships with others—neither greater, nor less than. Humility recognizes the unknown adventure of life. That it is possible, if I am really paying attention, that the next person I meet may become the best friend I ever have. Humility is the germ of awe.

Reflection Practice: How can I approach life in a more humble way?

MY REFLECTIONS:

Day 25

The Creativity of Being

"Being, or naked existence, is the one thing that we all are a part of. It seems the essential religious problem is that human beings suffer almost universally from a massive case of mistaken identity about their radical union with God. If we can break away from the illusion of our separateness then the rest follows rather clearly, and we can reconnect with our core identity. We are each a manifestation of that Universal and Divine Being, which then takes the form of angels, humans, animals, trees, water, and Earth itself."

Richard Rohr

A formula is emerging for us. It is the formula that underlies prayer practices throughout the centuries. We start from a perspective of humility. Sometimes we gain access to this perspective by having a wise mentor. We learn to be in an attitude of teachability with our mentor and gradually that perspective becomes the one with which we embrace the world. From a perspective of humility, we develop practices of gratitude. We do a daily gratitude list, or we start the day giving thanks for our lives, for our families, for our sobriety—whatever we hold dear. Then we learn to connect with ourselves and the world from an emotional place of thankfulness. We learn to extend energy into the world without having to have anything come back. We can do this if we feel grateful. If we feel deprived then it is almost impossible. We extend into the world from our emotional beingness.

Recently a friend told me that his bishop had preached a sermon in which he urged the congregation—not to be like Jesus, but to be Jesus. Being like—is to come from a less than place. If I want to be like Michael Jordan, I am saying to myself and the world that I am not him. I am affirming a kind of deprivation. In the realm of spiritual practices, as Obi Won said, there is no try, just do. Our spiritual task is to create from our beingness, to place our beingness into the world in a process of interactive creation. We don't pray to be more kind, or more like Jesus, rather prayer is an experiential realization in the body of a greater kindness, of becoming kindness. We can, the bishop urged, be Jesus. In the same way we can, by being the emotional experience of the Buddha, become the Buddha. It is what has gotten mystics in trouble with institutional authorities throughout history as they become what their intention has opened them up to be. This is difficult to understand because it is not either/or. We become Buddha-ness and we are not the Buddha. We become Jesus-ness and we are not Jesus, and we become kindness yet still have an identity besides kindness.

Reflection Practice: Am I willing to quit trying to be like something, or someone, and be willing to risk my beingness?

MY REFLECTIONS:

Day 26

Unity

"The Son is the image of the invisible God, the firstborn over all creation. For in him all things were created: things in heaven and on earth, visible and invisible, whether thrones or powers or rulers or authorities; all things have been created through him and for him. He is before all things, and in him all things hold together."

Colossians 1:15-17

From a perspective of humility and a heart full of gratitude, if we are concerned about peace we don't simply pray for peace, rather we allow our feeling state to expand into a feeling of peace. We become peace. We connect our intention with the emotional qualities of what we are praying for. In other words, it is not the power of positive thinking that does all the work, rather it is the power of our deep positive emotions that help us to interact with the world and participate in creating the reality we live in. It is the practice of bringing our emotional intention into congruity with our cognitive intention that opens the channel of connection of our beingness to the world.

The more strongly developed the emotional capacities of gratitude and connection, the greater the impact our emotional intention has on the world. We do not alone create our own realities, but our emotional intentions have a significant impact on our realities, and an even greater impact on the perspective from which we experience the reality in which we interact.

What Heisenberg showed on the subatomic level—that the charge of a subatomic particle depends on the point of view of the observer of the particle—we all know intuitively emotionally. If I emotionally feel lonely and isolated, I will experience the world as alienated from me. If I see the world as accepting and full of life, chances are I will experience myself in the world in a similar way.

Reflection Practice: Am I willing to take responsibility for how I help create the reality I live in? If I wish to change that reality am I willing to engage in practices that will give me the emotional capacity to do so?

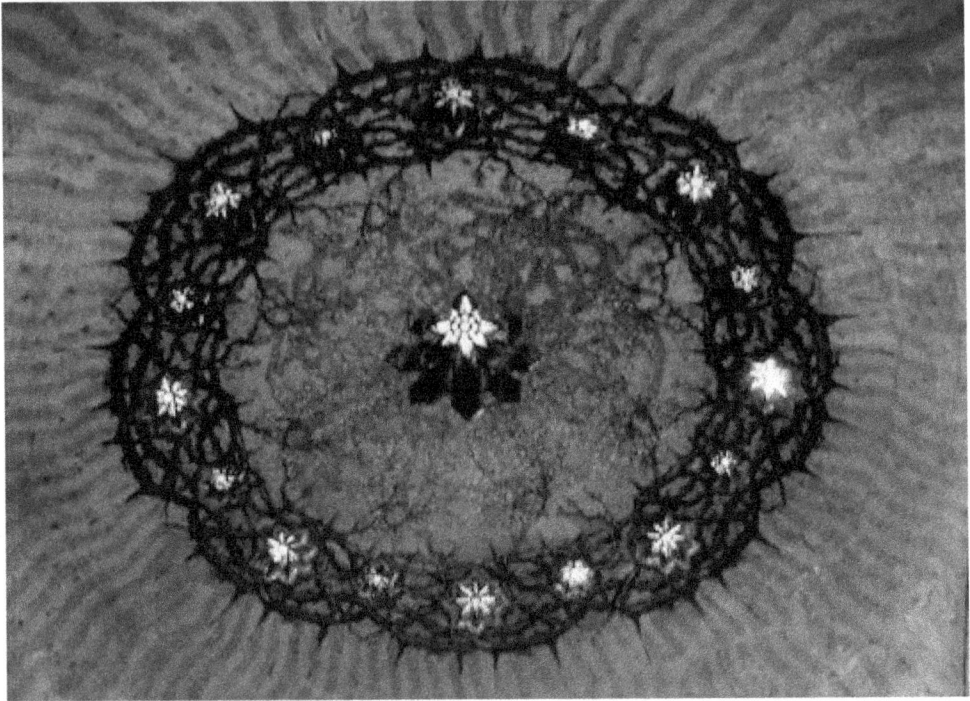

MY REFLECTIONS:

Day 27

Acceptance

"And if by grace, then it cannot be based on works; if it were, grace would no longer be grace."

Romans 11:6

A challenge we all face is how to get to, and stay in, the positive emotional place from which we connect with the positive energy of life. The quality of the way our energy relates to what is greater than us is determined by our emotional state. A primary way to enhance this state is from a perspective of humility and a practice of gratitude.

Still there will be times when more is needed. The context is that the ups and downs of life, the grief from losses, the anger from injustices all are ways in which our spiritual capacity is expanded, ways in which we grow in our ability to have compassion. Being in such growth passages is good, but it can also affect our outlook. The danger is that we can develop negative emotional patterns that prevent us from being in the positive emotional state by which our lives are vibrant and our life force strong.

This danger is resolved by learning acceptance. Acceptance, not as an intellectual understanding, but as an emotional practice. This is more subtle than it sounds. Acceptance is not repressing our negative emotions of sadness, anger, grief or the like. Acceptance is about feeling these emotions and letting their energy move and resolve. Acceptance is about the emotional process of acknowledging all aspects of what has happened.

On a societal scale it is like the Truth and Reconciliation Commission in South Africa. It is not a trial where justice or retribution is sought. It is bringing to light what, if left in darkness, would continue to carry seeds of conflict. In other words acceptance begins with the urge to get beyond the old polarities of right and wrong or victim and perpetrator.

Underlying acceptance is the understanding that somehow we are all connected in a web of life and that wishing harm to another harms ourselves.

Reflection Practice: Where am I stuck emotionally in an old pattern of resentment in my life? Am I ready to move beyond that?

MY REFLECTIONS:

Day 28

Beauty

"Now I walk in beauty, beauty is before me, beauty is behind me, above and below me."
Traditional Navajo Prayer

The practice of emotionally connecting to what is Greater, to God, to Beauty occurs through a perspective of humility and practices of gratitude. There is one other way this connection of gratitude has traditionally been fostered by all the great religious traditions—and that is through devotional practices. The Catholic and Orthodox traditions give us wonderful examples of this. A parishioner will focus on Mary or a particular saint (probably being drawn to that saint by projection—in other words that saint carries a quality that this person is trying to bring more into being in their own life) and becomes devoted to that figure. She will feel and develop love for the saint. She will light candles and say prayers to the saint. These devotional practices expand the emotional connection to the saint and to that aspect of God represented by the saint.

The same process is true in Hinduism, rich with devotional practices to various deities. What one is doing in the doing of these practices is strengthening emotional connection to something greater than self, outside of self. This often begins with a practice of devotion to a guru.

Tibetan Buddhism has many wonderful practices, many of which involve full body prostrations so the whole body is involved. This is helpful since emotions are bodily aspects, the more the whole body is involved in the devotional practice the more readily the sense of love and connection is felt. In Native American traditions many devotional practices involve devotion to Nature.

There is not much devotional practice in the West these days. It has an old fashion quality to it that our overly intellectual approach to life minimizes. We are afraid of being taken in by a guru and being betrayed by his floundering in some human way. Too many candles and too much incense can seem a little too primitive for many of us. Yet the practice of devotion may be one of the most effective ways to grow our emotional capacities to love.

Reflection Practice: What are the devotional practices that I might engage in that might most effectively help me practice care and love for something greater than myself?

MY REFLECTIONS:

Day 29

Cleansing Prayer

"The divine will is a deep abyss of which the present moment is the entrance. If you plunge into this abyss you will find it infinitely more vast than your desires," Jeanne Pierre de Caussade.

Prayer as a practice offers us two entirely different opportunities. Or perhaps said better, there are two very different practices, both of which are called prayer. The first is the practice of emotionally connecting to what is greater, to God, to divine Presence, to the experience of Beauty. We may use words to try to invoke an outer connection, but the goal here is first to have an inner emotional connection. This is the practice by which we stay in a perspective most open to life, where our energy will flow most freely, and we are least likely to get caught up in old survival defenses. This deep emotional practice is fostered by an attitude of humility and practices of gratitude. A second practice of prayer is emotional cleansing. When we connect to our inner self we may become aware that we are overwhelmed with sadness or resentment, or other lower state emotions. Our emotions can take us out of divine Presence just as quickly as a chattering mind. The practice here is one first of all of awareness. We must be aware of what we are feeling. Our feelings are the lights on the dashboard of our car of being. We have to become able to read the lights and understand what they mean. Once we are aware, our next task is acceptance. We must accept the reality of our feelings. We are often resentful that we feel resentful. What an emotional gordian knot of possibilities. What cuts through this knot is acceptance of the reality of the unpleasant emotion.

The third part of the cleansing prayer practice involves action. Usually there are several possible and often necessary actions. The first is simply to take a quiet moment to actually feel the negative emotion. Emotions are energy and once they are fully felt they usually will move on, dissipate on their own. That is unless they trigger some old wound, or engage some underlying pattern of vulnerability, which has shaped a lot of our life. Then the next action is to pray for the person or institution that seems to be the cause of what we are suffering. The usual recipe is to pray daily for ten days or two weeks. Often the emotion shifts after a day of prayer for the cause of our suffering. Sometimes we might end up praying for the cause of the suffering for thirty days or longer. In order for there to be effective emotional cleansing honesty is key. This means the prayer may start out. "Dear God please help that sorry s.o.b." There is no right or wrong way to make this prayer.

If we stick with it, if we continue to honestly feel and accept our emotions and pray for the cause of our suffering, our consciousness will expand. Emotionally there will be more room in our psychic house. Over time our cleansing prayer practice will free us.

<u>Reflection Practice</u>: Do I need a cleansing prayer practice?

MY REFLECTIONS:

Day 30

Prayer as a Practice of Holding Mystery

"We ought not to be weary of doing little things for the love of God, who regards not the greatness of the work, but the love with which it is performed."

Brother Lawrence

Our intention is important. The more we are able to live our intention in our minds and hearts, and the more we are able to live our intention open to the Mystery of life, the more likely we experience life in a profound and vital way. It may be apparent that there is a connection between this idea of holding our intention and prayer. In fact it might not be too far off to say that prayer is a way of holding intention. Brother Lawrence said centuries ago that prayer is nothing more than awareness. Add on to Brother Lawrence's comment and understanding that our most effective prayers are not mental at all, but come from our awareness at a deep place of emotional equanimity and centeredness. The power of prayer then is the power of our awareness open to a Mystery greater than ourselves. It is our way as humans to plug into the interconnectivity of all things and to come more into a place of our own truth in this web of life. Prayer is a practice that allows us to become our intention, plus the intention of the greater Mystery of life.

The recognition that prayer is a practice of holding intention at a mental, emotional, bodily and spiritual level allows us to look at it afresh as a way to grow and strengthen our lives. Today even the most dedicated humanist has to confront the realities of science which show us that the development of ideas, our mental intelligence alone, is not enough. We also need emotional intelligence. Science also shows us that if we stand in a certain way, or kneel in a certain way, or clasp our hands in front of our chest in a devotional way, that our very body postures in and of themselves engender certain emotional states. Prayer then is a practice of bringing into alignment our mental, emotional and bodily states in a way that is directed to something greater than ourselves. It is this other-directedness that gives prayer the quality of being a practice that moves us beyond the limits of our own desiring or contracting egos. Prayer is a practice for allowing us to move deeper and deeper into the profound Mystery and Beauty of life.

<u>Reflection Practice</u>: How might I open myself to a prayer practice today?

www.ingramcontent.com/pod-product-compliance
Lightning Source LLC
Chambersburg PA
CBHW080552030426
42337CB00024B/4841